S0-BCM-525

Sports Illustrated KIDS

BASKETBALL'S
BEST AND WORST

A Guide to the Game's Good, Bad, and Ugly

by
SEAN McCOLLUM

Sports Illustrated Kids The Best and Worst of Sports are published by
Capstone Press 1710 Roe Crest Drive, North Mankato, Minnesota 56003
www.mycapstone.com

Cataloging-in-Publication data
Name: McCollum, Sean, author.
Title: Basketball's best and worst : a guide to the game's good, bad, and
    ugly / by Sean McCollum.
Description: North Mankato, Minnesota : Capstone Press, 2018. | Series:
    Sports illustrated kids. The best and worst of sports. | Audience: Age
    9-14.
Identifiers: LCCN 2017047197 (print) | LCCN 2017048694 (ebook) |
ISBN 9781543506204 (eBook PDF) | ISBN 9781543506129 (hardcover)
Subjects: LCSH: Basketball—Miscellanea — Juvenile literature.
Classification: LCC GV885.1 (ebook) | LCC GV885.1 .M394 2018 (print) | DDC
    796.323—dc23
LC record available at https://lccn.loc.gov/2017047197

Editorial Credits
Nate LeBoutillier, editor; Bob Lentz and Terri Poburka, designers;
Eric Gohl, media researcher; Laura Manthe, production specialist

Photo Credits
AP Photo: Icon Sportswire, 21 (bottom middle); Dreamstime: Dgareri, 18
(bottom), Jerry Coli, 11 (top); Library of Congress: 4; Newscom: Cal Sport Media/
John Fisher, 18 (top), Icon SMI/Aaron M. Stprecher, 21 (bottom right), Icon
SMI/Chris Keane, 29, Icon SMI/John Biever, 13 (top), Icon SMI/Matt A. Brown,
7 (top), Icon SMI/TMB, 22, KRT/Harry Walker, 23 (top), MCT/Carlos Gonzalez,
21 (bottom left), Reuters/Sam Mircovich, 15 (bottom), TNS/Nhat V. Meyer, 5,
USA Today Sports/John E. Sokolowski, 17 (top), USA Today Sports/Kyle Terada,
28, USA Today Sports/Mark J. Rebilas, cover (left), USA Today Sports/Winslow
Townson, cover (right), ZUMA Press/Steve Lipofsky, 9 (right); Sports Illustrated:
Al Tielemans, 15 (top), Andy Hayt, 10, David E. Klutho, 19, John D. Hanlon, 16,
27, John Iacono, 7 (bottom), John W. McDonough, 9 (left), 11 (bottom), 12, 17
(bottom), 25 (top), Manny Millan, 13 (bottom), 20, 24, 25 (bottom), 26, Richard
Meek, 6, Robert Beck, 14, 23 (bottom), Walter Iooss Jr., 8, 21 (top)

Printed and bound in the United States of America.
010783S18

TABLE of CONTENTS

From Fruit Baskets to High-Flying Dunks

In December 1891, Dr. James Naismith was looking for a way to keep his college athletes in shape during the cold winter months. He had two peach baskets nailed to the balcony in a small gym. The first contest was nine-on-nine using a soccer ball. No dribbling was allowed. The peach baskets didn't even have the bottoms cut out. When a "goal" was scored, the janitor brought out a ladder to retrieve the ball.

And so basketball was born.

DEE-FENSE!!
DEE-FENSE!!

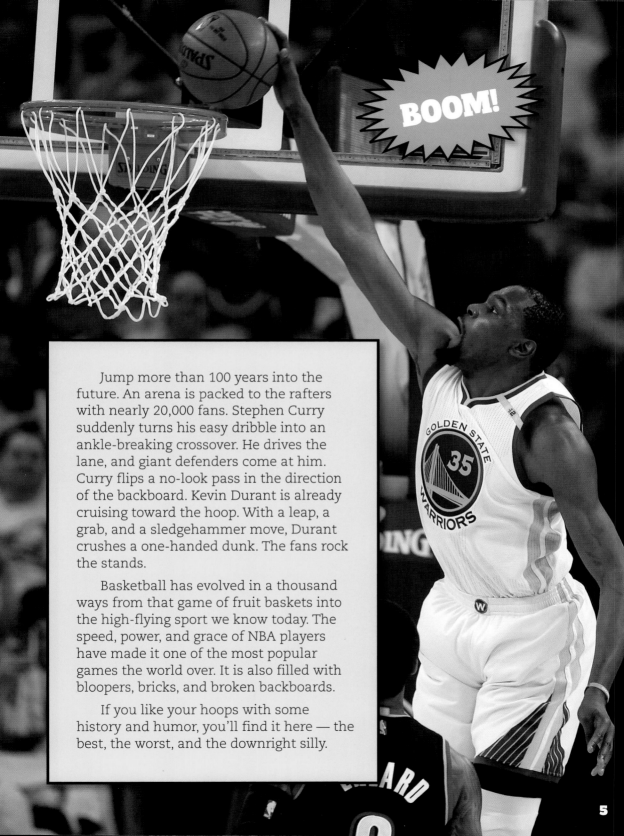

BOOM!

Jump more than 100 years into the future. An arena is packed to the rafters with nearly 20,000 fans. Stephen Curry suddenly turns his easy dribble into an ankle-breaking crossover. He drives the lane, and giant defenders come at him. Curry flips a no-look pass in the direction of the backboard. Kevin Durant is already cruising toward the hoop. With a leap, a grab, and a sledgehammer move, Durant crushes a one-handed dunk. The fans rock the stands.

Basketball has evolved in a thousand ways from that game of fruit baskets into the high-flying sport we know today. The speed, power, and grace of NBA players have made it one of the most popular games the world over. It is also filled with bloopers, bricks, and broken backboards.

If you like your hoops with some history and humor, you'll find it here — the best, the worst, and the downright silly.

CHAPTER 1

Defenders & Dunkers

Around the hoop is where big men patrol and NBA All-Stars fly.

DEFENDERS

"Defense wins championships." That's a favorite saying of hoops coaches. Here are three of the best shutdown defenders in NBA history.

Bill Russell

Bill Russell revolutionized NBA defense in the 1950s and 1960s. The Celtics center was plenty tall at 6-foot-10, but he was also quick and strong. He collected 21,620 career rebounds, including 51 in one game. He was also a master shot-blocker who turned the lane into a no-go zone. But the proof is in the jewelry. Russell helped the Celtics to 11 NBA titles in his 13-year career. In other words, he owns more championship rings than fingers to put them on.

BEST!

SWAT!

Hakeem Olajuwon

Hakeem Olajuwon was a great point producer, but his defense was all-world. He averaged nearly two steals and more than three blocks a game during an 18-year career, mostly with the Houston Rockets in the 1980s and 1990s. He was twice named Defensive Player of the Year and was also a nine-time member of the league's All-Defensive Team. He holds the the all-time NBA record for blocked shots.

Since his NBA debut with the Charlotte Hornets in 2005 **Chris Paul** has been a premier ball-handler and steady scorer. On D, he's also a picker of pockets, averaging nearly 2.3 steals per game (SPG). His SPG already ranks among the all-time defensive greats. He was traded to the Houston Rockets by the Los Angeles Clippers in 2017.

WORST!

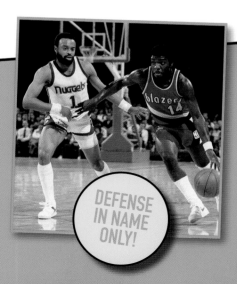

DEFENSE IN NAME ONLY!

Defense is also a team game. These three NBA squads had defenses that were downright offensive!

TEAM	YEAR	POINTS ALLOWED PER GAME
Denver Nuggets	1990–91	130.8
Denver Nuggets	1981–82	126.5
Seattle SuperSonics	1967–68	125.1

DUNKERS

Nothing brings a home crowd to its feet like a ferocious slam. Dunks are the game of basketball's emotional exclamation points.

BEST!

Julius "Dr. J" Erving turned dunking into an art form in the 1970s. As a forward on the 76ers, he possessed amazing speed and body control. In one of the most classic dunks ever, Dr. J turned a steal into a breakaway in a 1983 game. He cradled the ball in one arm and took off against the Lakers' Michael Cooper. He brought the ball around in a sick circle and slammed it home.

Michael Jordan is widely considered the greatest NBA player of all time. Among his talents was the ability to dunk over bigger opponents with his amazing hangtime skills. Jordan also twice won the NBA Slam Dunk Contest.

"Dr. J"

HELLO, MR. RIM!

LeBron James

BEST!

If a basketball genius was going to design the perfect NBA player, LeBron James would be the result. He is big and powerful with a lightning-quick first step. Nobody finishes a dunk with the authority of King James.

Darryl Dawkins was as big and strong as they will ever come. He got his nickname, "Chocolate Thunder," from music legend Stevie Wonder. In 1979, he shattered glass backboards in two games, sending pieces everywhere. "When I dunk, I put something on it," Dawkins said. "I want the ball to hit the floor before I do." Soon afterwards, the NBA switched to breakaway rims and shatterproof backboards.

KA-POW!

"Chocolate Thunder"

WHEN DUNKERS DON'T

How can you miss a dunk? It happens to best and at the worst times. Dunking legend Dominique Wilkins was playing in the 1991 All-Star Game and got out in front for an outlet pass. With nothing between him and the hoop, he brought the ball around for a windmill dunk. But he got too far under the basket and smacked the ball against the bottom of the rim. His All-Star buddies didn't let him forget it.

CHAPTER 2

Passers & Shooters

How do you beat the big guys? Pass around, dribble past, or shoot over them. Some players excel at disarming a defense.

PLAYMAKERS

Scorers get the glory, but good passers set the table.

"Magic" Johnson

Earvin "Magic" Johnson was huge for a point guard at the height of 6-foot-9. His size helped him see the whole floor and find the open man. He led his L.A. Lakers to five NBA titles in the 1980s.

John Stockton played his entire 19 years in the NBA with the Utah Jazz from 1984 to 2003. Teamed with Karl Malone, "Stock" averaged more than 10 assists per game. The pair's signature play was the pick-and-roll. Stockton would slash off Malone's pick and then flip the ball to the big man when Malone dashed to the basket. Stockton finished his career as the league's all-time assists leader with 15,806.

Rajon Rondo's highlight reel is a magic show. His passes seem to come out of nowhere. He helped lead the Celtics to a title in 2008 and has led the league in assists three times through 2017.

John Stockton

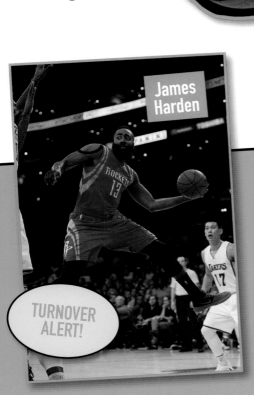

James Harden

TURNOVER ALERT!

In a 21-year career, Jason Kidd rose to second on the all-time assists leaderboard. However, he also ranks fourth all-time in turnovers. On November 17, 2000, while playing point guard for the Suns, he gave the ball away a record 14 times. Current Rockets star James Harden set his own greasy-fingered playoff record in 2015. He fumbled the rock to the Golden State Warriors 12 times.

SHARPSHOOTERS

The NBA first added the 3-point arc at the start of the 1979–80 season. The change inspired long-range shooters to take their best shot. Trifectas rank up there with dunks in bringing fans to their feet.

BEST!

Stephen Curry drained a remarkable 43.8 percent of his 3-pointers over his first eight seasons in the NBA. That sharpshooting helped him earn back-to-back MVP awards in 2014–15 and 2015–16.

His long-range daggers have also helped the Golden State Warriors win two NBA championships . . . so far.

MONEY IN THE BANK!

Ray Allen is a three-time winner of the The Sporting News' "Good Guy" award. He was also a 3-point assassin. He currently owns the NBA's all-time record of 2,973 treys in a career spent playing for the Milwaukee Bucks, Seattle SuperSonics, Boston Celtics, and Miami Heat from 1996 to 2014.

Steph Curry

BEST!

Steve Kerr was an important role player for the Chicago Bulls dynasty of the 1990s. He holds the highest career percentage for 3-pointers at 45.4 percent. Most recently, he's served as the head coach of 3-point savant Stephen Curry and the Golden State Warriors.

Steve Kerr

Charles Barkley

C'MON!

Stephen Curry will go down as one of the best 3-point shooters in NBA history. But for one night, his aim was epically ugly. In February 2017 against the 76ers, he missed all 11 of the shots he took from 3-point land. He blamed his inaccuracy on the weather. Really. The Warriors won anyway.

The worst all-time 3-point bricklayer? The case could made for Charles Barkley. The Hall-of-Famer tried 2,020 3-pointers in his career but only sank 26.6 percent.

FOUL SHOOTERS

Free throws are often the difference between Ws and Ls in tight games. It takes extraordinary inner-calm to sink the 15-foot shot with nobody guarding and everybody watching.

BEST!

Steve Nash knocked down better than 9 of every 10 free throws on average in his 18-year NBA career. One of his secrets was to practice his shot and follow-through on the line before the ref handed him the ball. He currently holds the all-time record for best free throw shooting percentage, having made 3,060 of 3,384 foul shots for 90.4 percent.

Steve Nash

BEST!

Mark Price ranks just a dash behind Steve Nash in career free throw accuracy at 90.38 percent. Stephen Curry again? Yep. And there's more to come. Curry currently ranks third all-time in free throw percentage. Teams try their best not to foul the "Baby-Faced Assassin" with the game on the line.

ALL BUT AUTOMATIC

FACT BREAK
For the 2008–09 season, Toronto Raptors guard José Calderón had an FT% of .981, an NBA record. At one point he hit 87 freebies in a row.

HACK-A-SHAQ

WORST!

Shaquille O'Neal

Shaquille O'Neal looked the part of Superman and was a huge, intimidating presence on the court. Free throws, though, were his Kryptonite. Shaq was only a 52.7 percent foul shooter. Those problems inspired teams to foul O'Neal without mercy. This strategy was named "Hack-a-Shaq."

Big **Ben Wallace** was a great defensive player and NBA champion. But he is still the NBA's all-time worst foul shooter with a career 41.4 free throw percentage.

DeAndre Jordan makes nearly 7 out of 10 shots from the field. But the All-Star center is an ironworker from the line. He is currently converting only 43 percent of his free throws.

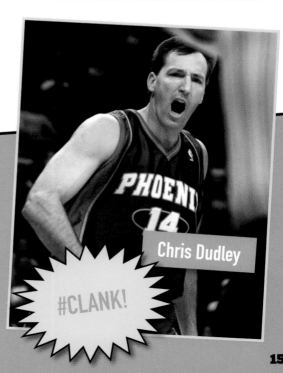

Chris Dudley

#CLANK!

Chris Dudley played for six different teams in a 16-year NBA career. But he was a terrible free-throw shooter with a herky-jerky style. He holds the NBA record for 13 misses in a row. In a 1989 game, he missed five free throws in one trip to the line. How? His opponents kept illegally stepping into the lane. The refs then had to let poor Dudley shoot again.

CHAPTER 3

Fun & Fashion

NBA players show more style than athletes in other sports. They've got the coolest nicknames, coolest shoes, and sometimes the coolest looks.

Wilt "The Stilt" Chamberlain

NICKNAMES

CLASSICS

- "Durantula" hints at the fear **Kevin Durant** strikes in opponents' hearts.
- Wilt "The Stilt" **Chamberlain** came by the name naturally as one of the NBA's first 7-foot giants.
- **David "The Admiral" Robinson** graduated from the U.S. Naval Academy. His leadership helped bring two NBA titles to the Spurs.
- For his hoop-crashing ways, **Blake Griffin** has earned the nickname "The Rim Reaper."
- **Giannis Antetokounmpo** was born in Athens, Greece, the son of Nigerian immigrants. His "Greek Freak" nickname honors his homeland, his rangy frame, and his sweet moves.

OFF-THE-WALL

- For his lanky looks, **Chris Bosh** was sometimes called "The Boshtrich."
- **Charles Barkley** used his wide body to control the low post and garner the nickname "The Round Mound of Rebound."
- What he lacked in flash, **Tim Duncan** made up for with mistake-free play. His mastery of the basic parts of the game earned him the nickname "The Big Fundamental."
- **Larry Johnson** became "Grandmama" after a series of 1990s TV commercials showed him rattling rims dressed as an old lady.
- "The Stifle Tower" refers to Frenchman **Rudy Gobert**. It shows pride in his home country as well as his shotblocking ability.

Giannis Antetokounmpo

THE COOL

BEST!

THE COLORFUL

Chris Andersen

STYLES

The NBA turned high-top, high-priced sneakers into high style. Nobody was more responsible for the fashion statement than **Michael Jordan**. His line of "Air Jordan" Nikes was launched in 1985.

He wore tattoos from his neck to his knuckles — plus a pointy Mohawk hairstyle. Truly, Chris "Birdman" Andersen has been one of the all-time colorful characters in the NBA.

Elbows fly in the NBA. In 2014 **LeBron James** sported a black carbon-fiber mask to protect a busted nose. The league asked him to replace it with a clear-plastic protector.

MASCOTS

Prancing and pranking, these puppet-like cheerleaders hustle to keep the crowd in the game. They are amazing athletes who pull off ridiculous stunts in ridiculous costumes.

BEST!

Bango the Buck risked his antlers to wow the crowd during a 2010 playoff game. The Milwaukee mascot did a backflip off a 20-foot high ladder. He dunked on his way down, landing back-first on a crash mat.

Bango

ROOF RAISERS

One of the freakiest mascot moments involved the Toronto Raptors' stuffed namesake. The dinosaur lived up to its ferocious reputation when it "swallowed" an entire cheerleader in its oversized suit.

Raptor

RAPTORS

BEST!

Sometimes mascots are downright heroic. In 2017 the Gorilla, a mascot for the Phoenix Suns, dove on the court during play. A drummer's stick had accidentally flipped onto the floor beneath the basket. Gorilla grabbed it and dove back, saving players from possible injury.

Gorilla

THAT COULD LEAVE A MARK!

The Utah Jazz wanted to honor the birthday of a season-ticket holder. Their Bear mascot showed up with a cake, birthday candles burning. By accident, it slipped off the tray and flew over the railing. The flaming cake dropped 30 feet to the seats below. Some fans got frosted, but no one was hurt.

To crack up fans in the snowy north, Minnesota Timberwolves canine mascot Crunch would zip down the stadium stairs on a plastic sled. Unfortunately, at a 2017 game, he smashed into a fan's knee. That fan was the dad of Karl-Anthony Towns, the Wolves' superstar center. The senior Towns later left on crutches.

UNIFORMS

Whether a team dominates or is enduring a losing streak, they can still look great. And there are always alternative and throwback jerseys to choose from.

LOS ANGELES LAKERS. The Lakers' intense purple and yellow stands out, and the look remains a classic. They flew these colors while winning a lot of games and multiple championships.

BOSTON CELTICS. Another old-fashioned style still worn by a world-class franchise. Why change greatness?

PORTLAND TRAIL BLAZERS. Portland, Oregon, takes great pride in its sole major-league sports franchise. The red, white, and black harmonize classically.

FACT BREAK
The NBA logo features the silhouette of Lakers Hall-of-Famer Jerry West.

OLD-SCHOOL FLAVOR

Who's playing tonight? Sometimes alternative and throwback jerseys can leave fans guessing. But as some of the uniforms age, they get cooler. Check out these unis and the teams they rep.

MINNESOTA TIMBERWOLVES

WASHINGTON WIZARDS

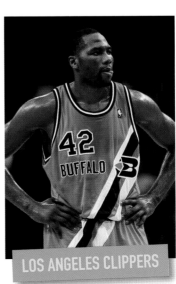

LOS ANGELES CLIPPERS

CHAPTER 4

Greats & Goats

ALL-TIME WNBA STARS

The Women's National Basketball Association (WNBA) hit the court in 1997. The best starting five of all time? Tough to do better than . . .

Diana Taurasi

BEST!

Diana Taurasi, Phoenix Mercury (Guard) Playing point or shooting guard, passing or driving, Taurasi is a defense destroyer. Taurasi is famous for her intensity, and currently holds the all-time WNBA record for points.

FACT BREAK
The WNBA season runs from May through September. The league began with 8 teams but now has 12, as several teams folded and others joined.

Sheryl Swoopes, Houston Comets/Tulsa Shock (Guard/Forward) She was the first player signed to an WNBA contract. All she did was immediately lead the Comets to the first WNBA title. Swoopes is a three-time league MVP with three Olympic gold medals to match.

Tamika Catchings, Indiana Fever (Forward) Catchings retired in 2016 as the league's all-time leader in steals and rebounds. She earned All-WNBA team honors 12 times. At the Olympics, she added four gold medals.

Sheryl Swoopes

Lisa Leslie

Lisa Leslie, Los Angeles Sparks (Center) Tall, fierce, and fearless, "Smooth" Leslie was one of the WNBA's first stars. She patrolled the paint blocking shots and snaring rebounds. She could score from inside and outside, earning three league MVP honors. In 2002 Leslie became the first woman to dunk in a game.

Lauren Jackson, Seattle Storm (Forward/Center) From Australia, "LJ" was a force in the middle for the Storm, leading the team to two championships. She used her height and muscle inside but was also accurate from the outside.

OFF THE BENCH:
Cynthia Cooper, Houston Comets
Teresa Weatherspoon, New York Liberty
Sue Bird, Seattle Storm
Yolanda Griffith, Sacramento Monarchs
Tina Thompson, Houston Comets

THE COACH:
Cheryl Reeve, Minnesota Lynx

COACHES

NBA head coaches make big decisions in split seconds that can win or lose a game. Fans remember the great calls. They never forget the bad ones.

LIFE IS GOOD!

Paul Westhead

It was Game 6 of the 1980 NBA Finals: Lakers vs. 76ers. The Lakers' great center Kareem Abdul-Jabbar was out with a bad ankle. Coach Paul Westhead surprised everyone by replacing Kareem at center with rookie point guard Magic Johnson. The strategy worked like, well, magic. Johnson put up 42 points, pulled down 15 rebounds, and dished out 7 assists. Most importantly, the strategy gave the Lakers a 123-107 win that clinched the championship.

BEST!

Gregg Popovich

Most NBA coaches are lucky if they survive three seasons. But Gregg Popovich of the San Antonio Spurs makes his own luck. His steady hand has led that team since 1996 . . . and counting. He has won NBA Coach of the year three times . . . and counting. As stars like David Robinson and Tim Duncan have gone and stars like Kawhi Leonard have risen, Pop has retooled teams to make the most of the team's strengths. That has added up to five NBA championships . . . and counting.

BAD DECISIONS

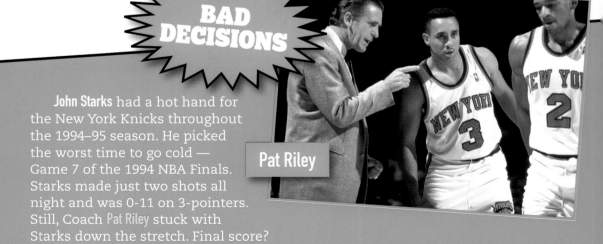

Pat Riley

John Starks had a hot hand for the New York Knicks throughout the 1994–95 season. He picked the worst time to go cold — Game 7 of the 1994 NBA Finals. Starks made just two shots all night and was 0-11 on 3-pointers. Still, Coach Pat Riley stuck with Starks down the stretch. Final score? Houston Rockets 90, Knicks 84. Long-time Knicks fans still feel the pain.

HISTORIC NBA SEASONS

The greatest of the great teams usually feature three things:

1) Selfless players who want to win more than be All-Stars. Great teams are often led by a guard who can pass and score off the dribble.

2) Big men who patrol the low post. They use their quickness and size to rebound, go strong to the basket, and back-stop on defense.

3) Sharpshooters. At least one long-range gunner who can make defenses pay if they clog the lane.

Michael Jordan

Dennis Rodman

BEST!
1995-96 Chicago Bulls, 72–10.

The first NBA team to reach 70 wins in a season, the Bulls were led by legendary coach Phil Jackson. They closed the deal by beating the SuperSonics in the NBA Finals, 4 games to 2.

Secrets of their success:

1. They ran the "Triangle Offense," a strategy that confused opponents. Different players rotated to play point guard.

2. Dennis Rodman averaged a ridiculous 15.6 rebounds a game.

3. Three players — Jordan, Steve Kerr, and Toni Kukoc — shot better than 40 percent on three-pointers.

LIFT, FLICK ...
SWISH!

BEST!

1971-1972
Los Angeles Lakers, 69–13.

Their season included a 33-game winning streak. After losing Game 1 of the NBA Finals to the Knicks, the Lakers reeled off the last four.

Secrets of their success:

1. Point guard Jerry West was 34 years old but was still the ultimate floor general. He averaged nearly 10 assists and 23 points per game.

2. The great **Wilt Chamberlain**, all 7-feet-1 of him, owned the glass. The big man pulled down 19 rebounds per game in the regular season, 21 during the playoffs.

3. Both West and shooting guard **Gail Goodrich** were sure shots from the outside.

Jerry West

BEST!

2015–2016
Golden State Warriors, 73–9.

Stephen Curry

The Warriors finished with the best regular season record ever. They cruised into the NBA Finals. There, they met the LeBron-led Cleveland Cavaliers for the second year in a row. (The Warriors had beaten the Cavs the year before.)

Up three games to one, the Warriors seemed to have a lock on a repeat. Then history happened. The Warriors lost, and the Cavs won, three games in a row. It was the first NBA Finals where a team had blown a 3-1 lead.

In 2016–17 the Warriors got revenge by topping the Cavs in the Finals, 4-1.

Secrets of their success:

1. No ball hogs. As a team, they moved the ball until they found the open shooter.

2. They played defense and rebounded as a team.

3. Paced by Stephen Curry, their .416 percentage beyond the 3-point arc was the second best in NBA history.

THE MOST FORGETTABLE SEASONS

WORST!

1972–1973
Philadelphia 76ers, 9–73.

The worst regular season in NBA history — a record no NBA team ever wants to break.

WORST!

2011–2012
Charlotte Bobcats, 7–59.

It could have been worse. The season had been shortened to 66 games due to labor problems.

WORST!

1947–1948
Providence Steamrollers, 6–42.

Talk about getting steamrolled. It is safe to say this season has been forgotten. Who even knew Providence, Rhode Island, ever had a pro basketball team?

ABOUT THE AUTHOR

Sean McCollum is a long-time sports fan who grew up hoping one day to play point guard for the Milwaukee Bucks. Alas, he proved too short and too slow. He turned to writing instead and has written more than 40 books for kids, tweens, and teens on everything from Theodore Roosevelt to werewolves to The World's Fastest Racecars. You can find out more about Sean's work at his website: www.kidfreelance.com.

GLOSSARY

assist — pass that leads to a score

center — position of a player who usually plays near the basket

dominate — to have control or power over

ferocious — very fierce or aggressive

forward — position of a player who plays both near and far away from the basket

guard — position of a player who plays farther away from the basket and is the primary ballhandler

intimidate — to make someone afraid

legend — a famous or important person who is known for doing something extremely well

low post — the area of the court under or just to either side of the basket

mascot — a person, animal, or object used as a symbol to represent a team and to bring good luck

rank — to place in a particular order

sharpshooter — a player considered to be a great shooter

title — the status or position of being the champion

READ MORE

LeBoutillier, Nate. *The Best of Everything Basketball Book.* Mankato, Minn.: Capstone/Sports Illustrated Kids, 2011.

Schaller, Bob. *The Everything Kids' Basketball Book: The All-time Greats, Legendary Teams, Today's Superstars—and Tips on Playing Like a Pro.* New York: Simon & Schuster/Everything, 2015.

The Editors of Sports Illustrated. *The Big Book of WHO Basketball.* New York: Time, Inc., 2015.

The Editors of Sports Illustrated. *Slam Dunk!: Top 10 Lists of Everything in Basketball.* New York: Time, Inc., 2014.

INTERNET SITES

Use FactHound to find Internet sites related to this book.

Visit *www.facthound.com*

Just type in 9781543506129 and go.

INDEX